SACRED SMOKE

SMUDGING:

An Ancient Art

For Modern Times

By

Harvest McCampbell

For All My Relations!

I would like to acknowledge my son Ezra and all my teachers, for being patient; Grandmother for introducing me to the Plant People, my Ancestors, and the Ancient Stories; Jana of Merry Meet Herb Shop for insisting; my sweetheart, Al Pierson for encouragement; and my friends and students, especially Jeffrey and Thea, for embracing the teachings of the Plant People and reflecting them back to me from a new perspective. I also wish to thank All My Relations, especially the Plant People for supporting me in my work. I will continue to do my best to support them in theirs. HO!

By The Same Author:

Women's Health Begins With The Moon

Published by Harvest McCampbell

First Edition
Copyright 1991 Harvest McCampbell.
Second Edition
Copyright 1992 Harvest McCampbell.

ISBN 0-9634065-0-7

TABLE OF CONTENTS

PUBLISHER'S NOTE: Smoke from herbs can cause allergic reactions, or trigger asthma and other respiratory distress. The following information is offered for its historical and cultural value. Neither the author nor the publisher assumes any responsibility for the way in which any individual responds to the smoke from any herbs. If you choose to burn herbs, please use common sense, and moderation. Discontinue use and see your doctor if any irritation develops.

SACRED SMOKE
SMUDGING: AN INVOCATION

first in quietness we light the candle
charcoal held between fingers or tongs
begins to crackle to sparkle

sacred herbs sprinkled
begin to glow
sacred fragrant smoke
spirals forward

inhale deeply
watching the smoke
spiral sky ward

the grandmothers
see them smiling
they watch us smiling prayerfully

prayerfully
we begin to sing
prayerfully to drum
prayerfully the healing is performed
prayerfully we sit in silence
alone with our ancestors
all of our ancestors

in beauty it is finished
in beauty it is begun
HO!

CREATION: SACRED HERBS

First Woman is Grandmother Spider. She Birthed Herself from the Void. It took a long time, a long, long time. It took eons of time. For She had nothing to work with except the Power of Her Own Thought. She Dreamed Her Thought into substance and as soon as She was Born She began to Spin.

She Wove the Sacred Spiral upon which the Universe was Born. Stars hung like Dew Drops on a Spider's Web in the Morn.

As soon as She finished, she traveled back to the Center, to the Vortex, to the Place where She was Born. And She began to Dance. She took the Sacred Rattles and Four Sacred Bundles out of Her Pouch. She Dreamed Herself Four Daughters, one Black, one Red, one Brown, one White. She placed one Daughter on each Bundle and Danced and Dreamed and Thought them Alive.

Grandmother Spider and Her Four Daughters Dreamed the Earth. When It was ready the Daughters came to Earth to Live. They became the Mothers of the first Human Families and the Sacred Grandmothers of the Four directions.

A long time passed. Grandmother Spider grew lonely for Her Children. She came to Earth as Thought Woman. After Wandering the Earth She Decided to Make a Home. She Built Her Lodge in the Forest near a Meadow where a Shaman and his Apprentice Lived.

She and the Apprentice became Lovers and together they had many Children. Eventually, a

5

drought came over the land and there was nothing to eat. Thought Woman's Children were crying because they were hungry.

She went to the Shaman and his apprentice and said "You must kill me so my children will not go hungry." At first they refused because they had both grown to Love Her.

She wandered around with Tears in Her Eyes looking for something for Her Children to eat. When She was sure She could find nothing She insisted "Kill me. It's the only way I'll ever be happy again."

When they finally agreed, She instructed them in how it was to be done. First they prepared a field by removing the rocks, and larger plants. Then they used their digging sticks to rough up the surface of the soil. Next they cut Thought Woman's Heart from Her Chest and planted it to the West of the field. Then they dragged Her Body across the field until all the Flesh was worn from Her Bones. Last, they planted Her Bones to the East of the Field.

When they were finished, the Thunder Beings came to mourn Her passing. Their Tears made the Land Fertile, Green and Magic.

From Thought Woman's Heart grew the first Oak Tree. It had Acorns of many kinds. From Thought Woman's Flesh grew Corn of many colors. And from Thought Woman's Bones grew the Sacred Herbs for Healing and Ritual. Along with the special Sacred Herbs to burn when we want Her to hear our Dreams.

SMUDGING

The burning of herbs or incense is a Sacred practice held in common by many traditions. In American Indian traditions we call this practice "smudging" or sometimes "smoking" even though the herbs may not be inhaled.

Smudging, practiced traditionally, takes many forms. Sometimes we tie the herbs in a bundle called a "smudge stick" and allow them to dry. There are some herbs that lend themselves to braiding, such as the Sweet Grass that you may have noticed in the movie "Dances With Wolves." In the Old Way, the end of the smudge stick or braid was lit from the council, central or cooking fire. Now we often use a candle. Matches aren't very efficient because it takes a while to get the stick smoking.

In some cultures, pinches or even branches of herbs are placed directly in a camp or council fire, or onto the burning wood in an indoor fireplace.

In other cultures, a coal is removed from the fire and placed in a special receptacle. The Sacred herbs (which are hung to dry and then crumbled) are sprinkled on the hot coal. This is the form most "new age" smudging takes today. Most people use prepared, quick-lighting charcoal. It's available from many Indian trading posts, at pow-wows, health food stores, new age shops, and even bible and Christian supply stores. (Smudging is similar to Catholic and Orthodox incense burning, for which bible and Christian supply stores carry prepared charcoal.)

The container used as a receptacle for your lighted charcoal and Sacred herbs needs to be fire-proof. Ceramic and glass bowls or abalone shells work well. There are also special chalices designed for smudging. Unless you use a chalice, place a layer of soil, sand or salt in the bottom for insulation, before adding your charcoal and herbs. The charcoal and smoldering herbs can heat the container up enough to scorch the surface it's resting on or the hand holding it.

If you prefer to light your whole bundle or braid, hold it in a candle flame until the smudge glows red. Blow out the flame; it should smolder at least a few minutes. You'll need a bowl or shell to catch the hot ashes.

When burning a bundle or braid of smudge they will eventually go out themselves. Should you need to put them out before they do, you can easily tamp them out as you would a cigarette or cigar. If you are burning herbs in a special receptacle, you can use a stick or spoon to gently tamp out the charcoal and herbs. The addition of a small amount of water also will do the trick, if you are in a hurry. Using water is messier, and considered a disrespect to the Fire Spirits.

The main idea behind burning herbs is to release their energy and fragrance, not to fill your room or your lungs with smoke. Burning excessive amounts of smudge or excessive burning of smudge can lead to respiratory distress, and other respiratory problems. A curl or two of smoke rising from your herbs is all that's necessary. If your eyes are burning, you're coughing or suppressing the urge to cough, you're either using herbs that don't agree with you or making way too much smoke. (Put out smudge, open the windows, leave the room and close the door.)

Show consideration for other people when burning smudge. Avoid burning smudge in the same room as infants, anyone who is pregnant, those suffering from respiratory problems, or those who have asthma or respiratory allergies.

To avoid fire hazards, never use smudge around flammable substances. And never leave burning smudge, charcoal, candles or fires unattended.

There are many Indian tribes, each with their own culture and belief systems. Not all tribes view the smoke rising from the herbs in the same light. And different herbs may be used for different purposes, depending on the person's tribe of origin.

Commonly, Sage, Sweet Grass and/or Cedar are burned to purify one's self, one's space and one's spiritual or healing tools. After lighting the smudge, we offer it to the cardinal directions, or hold it near our hearts. We wash or fan the smoke over our bodies by first bringing it towards the heart, then inhaling, pulling it up over the head, washing it down the arms, etc..

We also burn herbs during healing work and prayer. This helps one connect to their Spirit Helpers. The smoke carries ones intention to the Sky World, where the Spirit Beings and our Ancestors live.

During healing work, the smoke may be directed over your client by blowing, or fanning either with the hand or with feathers. This clears out old unhealthy energy and brings in the special attributes of the herbs.

RITUAL

Ritual is any action, undertaken with intention and belief that grows powerful through repetition and connection. The repetition can be personal, through this life time or many life times. It can be cultural, such as tooth brushing after every meal. Or it can be ancestral, such as the autumn dances held through out California by the Indians who have lived here for thousands of years.

Finding ones own personal ritual is a very healing experience. All rituals have a beginning point. Many traditional rituals began as dreams or visions. Often the ritual evolved out of the enactment of the dream or vision. Direct instruction for ritual sometimes came from Spirit helpers. This still happens today. It is possible that Spirit will instruct you through dreams or visions if you ask and open your heart.

Another way rituals evolve is by paying attention to ones feelings as one makes or attempts to make Sacred or Healing actions. The right actions feel good. A sense of well being and connection, of magic creeps into ones soul. Some people experience this quickly, but for others it evolves slowly. Patience and commitment are required as with any new endeavor.

Personal herbal rituals can evolve out of brewing tea or burning herbs. You can research how your genetic or spiritual ancestors used herbs. You can ask your family elders about various practices used in the past. You can read or take classes, using information while watching your feelings.

I gather herbs in a Sacred Way. With my intention made known to the plant, or following the plant's instruction to me. This act alone weaves me into the web of life and the universe. It connects me to both my ancestors and to all people and beings who have lived in a Sacred Way.

The ritual of gathering herbs in a Sacred Way is powerful healing for my soul. The time I spend in ritual with the Plant People sustains me through computer time and cement jungle time.

When you find your right and perfect ritual, I know it will sustain you too. Let the searching flow through your heart, let it be spontaneous. There is no exact recipe for your personal healing rituals, but with patience and commitment I know you will find them. HO!

NOTE: PREGNANCY is not a good time to begin experimenting with smudge. Most of the herbs can cause miscarriage in people whose bodies are not familiar with their use. If you become pregnant, moderate or stop your use of smudge. Avoid inhaling it directly or avoid it entirely. If you are having trouble getting pregnant, you might want to avoid smudging for a few months just in case it may help.

MY FAVORITE HERBS FOR SMUDGE

CALIFORNIA BAY (Umbelluaria californica):
Last summer, my sweetheart and I were in the mountains gathering herbs in a Sacred Way. I observed him in conversation with a Bay tree. I was surprised at their agreement on the amount of leaves to be gifted and accepted. Later, I asked what he was going to do with all the Bay leaves. "I'm going to use them for smudge." I didn't think that was traditional, and told him so. He didn't care what I thought. It was between him and the Bay. As it turned out, within a few days, I accidentally ran across a reference to California Indians' traditional use of Bay leaf smudge in the autumn to protect against colds and flu!

CEDAR, CYPRESS, JUNIPER, (Various botanical names.): We use these conifers to consecrate or make Sacred. You can smudge yourself, your space, tools, and clients. The fragrance is both calming and uplifting. Many people connect with their guidance and Spirit Helpers when using this smudge. I prefer the California Incense Cedar because of my special relationship to the plant and its spirit. The first time I went to the woods to gather smudge, I was hoping to gather Cedar and Desert Sage in a Sacred Way. I wasn't really sure where they grew. I followed my heart for miles and hours longer than I had intended to drive. When I finally found the right place to stay for the night, it was well past midnight. I promptly crawled into the back of my little blue truck and went to sleep. In the morning I found myself parked under a California Incense Cedar. The Sage was growing all around. I gather Cedar both from my special wild places, and from places that call to my heart. I always ask and only take a little from each plant, with thankfulness!

FENNEL (Foeniculum vulgare): Europeans have used this herb for food, medicine and to repel evil energies since the middle ages. It can be incorporated with other herbs to burn as smudge, hung over the door, near the bed, or carried in a small medicine pouch. Fennel can be gathered from the wild. The flowers, seeds, stalks or leaves are equally effective used as smudge. Be aware that it looks similar to Poison Hemlock. And the two are often found growing side by side. (See Publishers Note, page 3.)

MEXICAN TEA, OR EPAZOTE (Chenopodium ambrosioides): Epazote helps one to establish healthy boundaries. When as a result of abuse or poor self-esteem you have pulled in on your self, or have given up your boundaries entirely, Epazote can be helpful. Its energy is about establishing flowing boundaries that respond to the environment. Try a bundle by your bed or a pinch in your smudge pot. Native to the Yucatan, it's believed to have established itself in California without human intervention. Given the number of uses for which natives of the Yucatan employ Epazote, and the high population of Mexican Americans in California, I am not so sure. I am glad that it chooses to share this environment, so I can accept its Medicine Gift.

MINT (Mentha, Monarda various species): The Mints are both cleansing and uplifting. They can be burned either alone or incorporated with other herbs. My preference is to add a small amount of mint to my basic Cedar and Sage mixture. I use either a sprig or two of wild mint or prunings from those grown in my yard. (See Publishers Note, page 3.)

MUGWORT (Artemisia vulgaris): A California native, with similar species found in many parts of the world. It is used for healing, divination, and to stimulate dreams and visions nearly everywhere it occurs. I was once showing a friend my plants and herbs when she asked "Do you have Mugwort growing here by your door?" "Yes a little bit, but I keep pulling it out, I have more over here beneath my bedroom window." "Oh, you shouldn't pull it out! It wants to be here. In European tradition, it is called Cronewort, and they say it likes to grow at the doors of healers." Mugwort bundles can be hung by your bed, or burned before sleep or during ritual. Some people find the smoke to be slightly mind-altering. As with any mind-altering substance avoid its use if you plan on driving, operating machinery, or have an infant or other dependent person in your care. I gather my Mugwort, with care and respect, from wild plants, or from the special ones beneath my window when they need to be trimmed. UNSAFE FOR PREGNANCY.

14

MULLEIN (Verbascum thapsus): Mullein grows wild over much of the industrialized world. Its special spiritual work is to heal the damage created by human activity. It is not uncommon to see a large plant growing where a recent road cut fords a stream. The mullein stands ready to cast its seeds upon any subsequent erosion. Not only will the roots help to hold the soil in place, but the furry leaves attract and hold dust and wind-blown soil. Mice and insects find shelter, food and protection under the spreading leaves of the mullein plant. Not only are the leaves eaten by many creatures, but the nectar from the flowers and the copious supply of seeds provide for many. Life encourages life. The waste products of the mice and insects enrich and rebuild the soil. Given time, mullein and her helpers will heal the damaged land.

The work mullein has to do in the wild is very important. I am careful not to interfere out of selfishness or self-centeredness. When I collect mullein from the wild I take only a single leaf from each plant, after seeking each plants' permission. I bundle my leaves together, often using four leaves, one for each direction.

I burn a pinch or two at a time either on charcoal, or by holding a leaf so that a small surface rests in a candle flame. I inhale the smoke, and direct it to my heart or the area of myself or my client that needs healing. I use it for healing trauma that originates out of relationships with other people, or for protection in new endeavors. Most people find the smoke to be very grounding and calming. (See Publishers Note, page 3.)

PINE, FIR, HEMLOCK, SPRUCE (Various botanical names): These conifers are burnt for their purifying and cleansing effect. I often gather a shoot or two from the trees growing near where I am collecting herbs, or use the prunings from trees growing in my yard. Many people use Pine, especially Pinion Pine, alone. I sometimes incorporate Pine, Fir, Hemlock, or Spruce with the other herbs I'm using for smudge.

RESIN, BALSAM, GUM, SAP (Various origins): I gather dried droplets of resin from various forest trees to use for smudge and healing. I never collect the sap that is closing a wound, and I try to avoid any that is still gooey. I am partial to resins from pine, juniper, fir, and spruce trees. People also use sweet gum, birch and acacia, among others. Some examples of commercially available resins are benzoin, copal, dragon's blood, frankincense and myrrh. Resins embody the four elements when used as smudge or incense. Water is pulled from the Earth by the trees' roots and transformed into sap. The tree grows from Mother Earth to Father Sky, offering its fragrance to the realms of both Sky and Earth. The sap as resin embodies the elements of Earth and Water and their movement towards the Sky. When burning we introduce the element of Fire, and as the resin transforms into smoke, it becomes Air. Symbolically and actually, we are affirming and partaking of our connection to all creation when we prayerfully inhale the Sacred Smoke of our chosen resin. (See Publishers Note, page 3.)

SAGE, DESERT (Artemisia tridentata): This plant is called Sage Brush, Black Sage (for its seeds) and White Sage (for its appearance). It is used interchangeably with various other Artemisias and Salvias for their ability to clear both negative and foreign energy and entities from oneself, one's environment, or one's tools. My connection with Desert Sage is my connection to my spirituality and my personal growth. My first affirmation came with a gift of a dried and pressed sprig. Every time I smelled that sprig, and indeed every time I smell Desert Sage, I am reminded that "I am all right, right now!" (Remember, all there is, is now!) As with all the herbs I gather, I proceed in a Sacred Way with respect and thankfulness.

SWEET GRASS (Glyceria fluitans, G. aquatica, Hierochloe odorata): This wild grass is found growing on the plains of the U.S. and Russia. We use the smoke for grounding, protecting and making Sacred. It's used alone or in combination with Cedar and Sage. (See Publishers Note, page 3.)

UVI URSI (Arctostaphylos uva-ursi): The fragrance and energy of this herb is very calming and grounding. It is one of the herbs commonly mixed with Tobacco and called Kinnikinnink. This blend is often used for smoking during Pipe Ceremony.

WILD TOBACCO (Nicotiana various species): When Grandmother Spider grew lonely for her children, She was born as Thought Woman from a dewdrop resting on a Tobacco leaf. Ever since, Tobacco has been used to connect with Sacred Beings and Wisdom. Unprocessed Tobacco is smoked, used for smudge, put in medicine bags, and kept with tools. We often employ it whenever Sacred energy is needed.   (See Publishers Note, page 3.)

YERBA SANTA (Eriodictyon californicum): Yerba Santa, or The Saints Herb, is a California native. A traditional smoking and smudging herb, it has also been used medicinally for a number of complaints, both internal and external. Unlike Mullein, Yerba Santa does not follow people's footsteps. The places Yerba Santa chooses to grow tend to have an ancient Sacred feel about them. When people encroach on its territory, by making roads or other construction, it responds by carrying on as best as it can. It tends to hold its own ground until the energy or the environment has changed drastically. When all the wildness is gone from a place, it is very rare to find Yerba Santa. Burn or carry Yerba Santa to nurture and protect that which is ancient, Sacred and wild within your self. Use it when you need encouragement to hold your own ground and for courage when the time for retreat is at hand. I collect Yerba Santa from large stands and only one sprig or a leaf or two from each plant. I first talk to the plant, listening for any special instructions it may offer me. When there are none I make sure the plant agrees to the use for which I am gathering.   Ho!

BUYING HERBS FOR SMUDGE

Most people who smudge purchase their herbs from health-food stores, herb shops, new-age shops, trading posts, or from vendors at pow wows, rendezvous, or Indian and Mountain man shows. Herbs that are not gathered and prepared for smudge are not preferred, but are acceptable. When you get them home, place them on your altar or other special place. Invite the Spirit of the Herb(s) to join you and guide you in your Sacred Work.

Whether you speak to them silently through your heart or aloud, is up to you. Do whatever makes the process seem the most real. Use respect, kindness and affection when addressing the Spirit of the Herb(s). Consider having the intention to form a long-lasting friendship and partnership.

Your intention will be known. If you merely wish to use the herbs, rather than become their partners, the herbs probably will stay "dead" or their energy may withdraw. Part of the Spiritual Work of the Plant People is to work with Human Spirits. When we have the intention to become partners, much more of their magic manifests in our lives.

If you want to purchase herbs that have been gathered in a Sacred Way, ask "Who gathers these herbs and how is it done?" Check around, you'll eventually find a source that feels good to your heart and Spirit. See ABOUT THE AUTHOR, page 20, if you want to learn to gather your own.

BIBLIOGRAPHY

The herbs I've shared are all long-time friends of mine. I used the following books for botanical names, to jog my memory, or to give physical-world confirmation to what I knew from Spiritual sources. **"SUNSET'S NEW WESTERN GARDEN BOOK"** for botanical names; **THE AUDUBON SOCIETY POCKET GUIDE - FAMILIAR TREES OF NORTH AMERICA** for botanical names, (good for identification); **AN ETHNOBIOLOGY SOURCE BOOK** part of a 20 - volume series, Garland Publishing, Inc. This is the book containing the reference on California Bay. I also used it for botanical names, memory jogging and confirmation. This book is very informative, but it is difficult to use and even harder to find.

ABOUT THE AUTHOR

Harvest McCampbell is a healer, teacher, artist and poet of Northern European and American Indian descent. She has lived and worked in Northern California for over 17 years. You may contact Harvest for information on healing sessions, classes, her quarterly newsletter "Finding Your Way With Herbs" and her home-study course on Spiritual Herbology. Harvest also leads retreats once a year to introduce people to smudge herbs in their natural settings. For information send a S.A.S.E. with a note on what information you're interested in to Harvest McCampbell, 7737 Fairoaks Blvd. #201, Carmichael CA 95608. (916) 558-0497